D1270719

ACCESSIBILITY

DISABLED WORLD TRAVELS

Tips for Travelers with Disabilities

By Tracey Ingram, M.A., M.S.

Accessibility: Disabled World Travels – Tips for Travelers with Disabilities

ISBN: 9780999577547
Library of Congress: 2018905172

Publisher: Sovereign Education Media
332 S. Michigan Avenue Floor 1032
Chicago, IL. 60604 USA
sovereigneducationmedia
312 685-2788

Jacket design: GermanCreative
Cover Image: Orange Blue Studio/Shutterstock.com
Image Inside Book: iQoncept/Shutterstock.com

TABLE OF CONTENTS

Follow me on Facebook:

@Travelers with Disabilities

Check out Authors Blog: Travelingbarrierfree.com

TESTIMONIALS

5.0 out of 5 stars

A gem for those with disabilities or those traveling with the disabled, May 22, 2013

ShyGal "avid book reader" (Colorado) - **Amazon Verified Purchase**

This short guide is a quick read that is nevertheless packed with useful tips for the disabled who wish to travel or those traveling with the disabled. The author first gives an excellent overview of the definition of the term "disabled," then reviews how the tips in the guide will specifically help. Benefits include how to have your assistant travel for free, how the visually-impaired can see better on trips, and so forth. At first, I was a little doubtful. I have quite a bit of experience as the traveling companion of my elderly great aunt, and I thought the list of benefits was a little overblown. But then I read through the rest of the book and thought the tips to be very helpful, well-researched, and true-as-promised. The book has checklists for each section that helps the traveler determine what kind of trip they want to have and then proceeds to offer checklists to help the traveler prepare for the trip so that the trip turns out just as desired. Having been so well-traveled as a companion, even I was surprised by the nuggets of knowledge and resources offered--everything from TSA rules and regulations to organizations dedicated to swapping lodgings that are fully accessible for all kinds of disabilities. The guide even tells you how to travel with wheelchairs, canes, and so forth. It's pretty detailed, very accurate, and should offer a great deal of freedom to those want to travel in spite of disabilities. Wish I had this book earlier on in my travels with my great aunt!

5.0 out of 5 stars **Nice overview of travel tips for various challenges!**, July 28, 2013

Rik Isensee (San Francisco, CA) **Amazon Verified Purchase**

Tracey has provided a concise overview of various considerations the disabled traveler is wise to check on before heading out -- starting with the nature of one's own disability, and what your special requirements are. She covers mobility devices, hearing and visual impairments, tips for handling oxygen, medications, and service animals, with checklists for each one. She also provides an extensive list of resources, including how to contact TSA, accessible cruises, and travel agents who specialize in smoothing the way for people with disabilities.

One of my own visually-impaired clients pointed out that even so-called "able-bodied" persons are really TABs: Temporarily Able-Bodied, as aging and infirmity in various forms eventually come to us all (if we're lucky!).

A very-much needed resource for an increasingly aging population that still wants to get out there and experience the world! Tracey shows us how.

5.0 out of 5 stars **Very Helpful**, July 24, 2013

Cynthia Carr - **Amazon Verified Purchase**

I purchased this book because I have a number of friends and people in our ministry with handicaps and we frequently have to travel together and I need to be able to help them in new places. Most of them have learned how to be prepared for these situations, but some are not aware of the resources available to them. I especially enjoyed reading about some of the new technology such as the Pebble for the visually impaired and software that will enlarge the computer print. There were also lots of good tips when traveling to new places such as writing down the address or directions to the place you are traveling, not for you to read, but in order to ask directions. Also had a good list of resources to call or visit for disability information before traveling. I am recommending this to our friends and members with disabilities.

5.0 out of 5 stars **Useful and Timely Resource**, July 21, 2013

Fleury M. Sommers "Avid Reader" (Houston, TX USA) **Amazon Verified Purchase**

This is an extremely useful and - at least for me - timely book to have on my shelf. It's essentially a well thought out and well researched guide for traveling with a variety of disabilities, all of which present their own unique challenges.

The author is an expert in the area. She is a therapist who specializes in this subject, so this isn't an internet marketer trying to cash in on a niche. (To me, this is important because it exponentially increases the effort of the author in developing the book and in consequence the value she delivers on a subject that affects not only quality of life but emotional well-being.)

The author also repeatedly asks her readers to send her traveling tips she may have overlooked. I hope people do. As our parents get older and as we get older, the subject becomes more and more relevant.

If you need this kind of advice, don't hesitate to buy the book.

Fleury Sommers

5.0 out of 5 stars **Disabled World Travels ... - Tracey Ingram**, June 17, 2013

S. ROYSTONE NEVERSON (Trinidad And Tobago, Caribbean) **-Amazon Verified Purchase**

If you are disabled or has a family member who is disabled, or work with disabled people, this is a very useful book to have when traveling is involved. It is well researched. It tells you how to plan you travel, provides you with the important questions you should ask of yourself as well as of the agency that is providing the service.

Additionally, the book puts you in touch with the experience of other disabled persons so that you could benefit from their experience.

Of special interest is the section dealing with how to avoid special needs problems. The author also throws in an invaluable special checklist.

5.0 out of 5 stars **This is a must read for disabled travelers**, May 22, 2013

FLAV - See all my reviews

This review is from: Disabled World Travels (Kindle Edition)

Kudos to this author for sharing such useful information. Highly recommend this read to anyone who has travel plans coming up if you have any kind of mobility issue or other disability. I like the way the book was organized and think the information is really useful. The checklists alone are worth the download.

5.0 out of 5 stars **Great Resource For Travelling With Disabilities**, May 21, 2013

Darrin Wiggins - See all my reviews

Amazon Verified Purchase

I would say Disabled World Travels is one of the most comprehensive resources on traveling with disabilities that I have ever seen. Having had an elderly mother in-law that had mobility issues I can appreciate the checklists that are provided in the book. When you are free to come and go with ease you stop appreciating what you have and take it for granted. This book provides you with great reminders of what to look and ask for when travelling.

The resources in the back of the book shows the author has taken the time to do the proper research and wants to make a difference for people traveling with disabilities. I would recommend this book for anyone traveling with disabilities and for anyone who may be traveling with someone that has disabilities. By using the information provided you will be capable of making travelling that much more enjoyable.

5.0 out of 5 stars **There's a great need for this book.**, May 20, 2013

Marcus Chacos - **Amazon Verified Purchase**

As a health care practitioner I often have clients with disability. I also have family members with age related disabilities... and this book is the perfect resource to add both comfort and practicality to their travel needs as well as adventure to their (often restricted) travel opportunities.

The book helps define disability and discusses travel hints for elements such as mobility devices, oxygen and medications as well as considerations for sight and hearing impaired travelers.

Overall, if you are travelling with any disability or are traveling with someone who is... this book is for you!

5.0 out of 5 stars **A Valuable Resource**, May 15, 2013

Shmaya David "eCoachingSuccess" (Israel) -**Amazon Verified Purchase**

This book is a valuable resource for people with disabilities and their companions. It will also be valuable for therapists and coaches working with the disabled, and for anyone whose job involves planning travel for others, such a tour guides, reservation offices, in-house corporate travel coordinators etc.

The book begins with general ideas and suggestions on how to plan your travel. Than, every chapters tackles a different challenge and gives the reader good advice on how to prepare for travel and what to do in different situations. It also guides the reader to the best approach to take in various situations, and there are also checklists to use for planning and preparing in a way that will minimize problems.

Tracey Ingram, M.A., M.S.

The book includes information about legal requirements concerning service providers. When all else fails, the book tells you how to stand up for your rights, both immediately and when you may need to file a complaint later on.

Introduction

Have you ever felt ignored or received poor treatment when you traveled? Do you feel inspired or intimidated when you think about traveling? Do you still want to travel but feel that your disability limits you?

According to the World Health Organization, approximately 15% of the world's population lives with some form of disability and 2-4% experience significant difficulty in functioning. This estimate is likely to be understated and is increasing due to the aging population and the rapid epidemic of many chronic diseases.

The word disabilities imply impairments, limitations of activity, and some restrictions. Some people think when they hear the word "disabilities" it means the person is confined to a wheelchair. This is totally false. When a person is impaired this suggests there is a problem in body function or structure which may be temporary or permanent. Activity limitations include difficulties encountered by an individual when engaging in a task or action. A participation restriction is a problem experienced by an individual when involved in life situations such as not being able to play tennis or climb stairs.

The term "disabilities", is very complex because it involves the individual with a disability and how society reacts. People with disabilities have the same health needs and rights as non-disabled people, however evidence suggest that people with disabilities face many barriers in accessing the health and services they need.

The author, an experienced Occupational Therapist and Clinical Audiologist has witnessed firsthand situations that people with disabilities have been discriminated against and treated poorly. An occupational therapist is interested in the ability of any individual to participate in meaningful life endeavors such as traveling, despite the existence of any dysfunction. This series was created as a result of worldwide travel encounters with people who have a wide variety of disabilities, clinical experiences, and hours of research.

This travel series is divided in chapters which outlines specific disabilities and challenges and then reveals some of the solutions to have a more successful journey. Each volume of the series will have an accessible travel resource list which is accurate at the time of printing; however policies and procedures can change. Be sure to check with the resource of interest for the most updated information. If you have a favorite resource that has been helpful please feel free to share the information so it can be added to the resource list for the next series.

Anytime you are doing business with a company it is important to do your own research to make sure that your specific needs will be met. Write down or record questions that you want to ask the service provider prior to talking with them. This is written as an educational series however does not imply medical advice. It is very important to discuss with your physician prior to making any concrete vacation plans for advice about your medical needs. Some of the specific disabilities discussed in the first volume of the series include tips for the visually impaired, hearing impaired, wheelchair accessible solutions, traveling with mobility issues, traveling with oxygen, traveling with medications, and more!!

The first volume of the series will teach you the principles I've shared with others to do the following:

- How hearing impaired people can enjoy enhanced clarity with speech.

- Be informed and have less stress with travel preparations.

- Low vision travelers experience increased visual acuity.

- Discover how to enhance your lip-reading and listening skills.

- Easier accessible travel with less fatigue.

- How to enjoy traveling with oxygen without fear.

- Swap and rent accessible homes worldwide.

- Join a free club that will deliver your luggage to your destination.

- Arthritis sufferers discover tips to relieve arthritic symptoms.

- Diabetics find out the latest American Diabetes Association's guidelines on exercise.

- Hearing impaired? Get a Free caption phone with free delivery and setup.

Check out the Author Travel Blog: travelingbarrierfree.com

Disabled World Travels

CHAPTER 1: LIVING WITH A DISABILITY

Currently, there are over 500 million people worldwide and 57 million people living with disabilities in the United States, meaning that roughly 1 in 5 Americans are living with a disability. (Source: 2000 census). CNN reports that approximately 21 million American families include at least one member with a disability, and over 65 million Americans are caring for family members with disabilities. Between 1990 and 2000, the number of Americans who have disabilities increased 25%, according to the Disability Funders Network.

According to the Americans with Disabilities Act (ADA), an individual with a disability has a temporary or permanent physical or mental impairment that substantially limits at least one or more life activities, such as being able to breathe, walk, see, hear, and other performance skills.

Travelers with disabilities cannot afford to be carefree as their able-bodied friends when making travel arrangements. Travel for disabled people can be filled with additional challenges and requires serious planning. Unfortunately, many locations don't provide the same quality of special needs services.

It is critical for travelers with disabilities to foresee their special needs in detail to ensure those needs are met throughout their journey to maximize comfort. You will want to plan, verify the details, and check again. Many travelers simply rely on special travel agencies that cater to those with disabilities. It is also important that when things go wrong in your journey that you know your rights and how to protest.

Through the resources in this book, you will be able to access the disabled travel community who has written reviews describing their best and worst holidays worldwide. This allows you to choose where you want to go and what to avoid. There are wheelchair accessible adventures in Bali,

New Zealand, Portugal, Switzerland, and the United States. The forums and social interaction with other travelers with disabilities are helpful when planning and can help you make some important decisions.

What type of vacation do you want?

The Realities of Planning

Regarding accessibility, the United States has set the standard for physical access. You have the right to go anywhere in the world. Some people like rugged trips and others are looking for something similar to what they will find in the United States. If you are interested in traveling outside of the country with a disability or other mobility challenges you must plan for any number of contingencies.

It is important to investigate the country you are thinking about visiting to learn about the laws and the culture of the country. Countries that have signed and ratified the United Nations convention on the rights of Persons with Disabilities with some countries having ADA equivalent regulations are listed here: The Travel list. In the resource section, I have a list of international countries and domestic U.S. cities that travelers who are in wheelchairs have personally listed as wheelchair friendly. When you are traveling, it is important to be flexible. If you are not traveling with a group tour, look for disability organizations or resources at your destination and some local contacts.

Be sure to research the countries you are planning on visiting. Learn the foreign vocabulary and review the cultural differences before you leave is important. Have a backup plan and bring along items such as a portable ramp, a reacher, and other items you need to make yourself comfortable.

Travel Insurance

Traveling is filled with uncertainty, and no one wants to get sick or become ill on vacation. You may consider getting travel insurance that covers pre-existing conditions and medical evacuation insurance when you are traveling abroad.

Travel insurance is a good option to consider if you suspect you may cancel the trip or feel that you may need international healthcare on the trip. Medical evacuation insurance is helpful should you need treatment abroad and need to fly back to your hospital of choice in the U.S. If you are using a travel agency don't buy travel insurance from them. If they go out of business, there may not be any money left over to cover your claim.

When shopping for insurance, you want the widest amount of options to review. Check out Insuremytrip.com for a website that lists more than 100 plans from 18 providers. For more details and examples of pre-existing condition coverage, you will want to visit the travel insurance review group. Travel Insurance Review has been around for many years and has a lot of helpful information on their website that offers an unbiased review of the industry.

What type of trip interests you? Are there specific places you dream about? Make a list and prioritize. What is your overall budget? Be realistic. Are you seeking trips with other travelers who have disabilities? Will you be traveling with your caregiver or family? Are you a senior who wants to travel with other mature adults of the same age group? Thinking about a cruise? Does a safari sound like fun to you? The possibilities are endless. Try not to limit yourself or feel trapped by your medical diagnosis; however, it's important to do a personal self- assessment and meet with your physician and discuss on your daily mobility requirements, medication needs, and many other issues before you select that final destination.

Mobility Requirements

What are your daily and weekly mobility requirements? Traveling offers so many exciting opportunities to see and experience different cultures, catch up with friends and family, and to simply relax. It also represents a complete break from your normal daily routine and schedule. This break from your schedule can be a welcomed relief or very stressful for others.

If your daily mobility requirements at home are difficult traveling in unfamiliar environments can potentially make you feel uncomfortable. To reduce this feeling try to plan as much as possible by working with specialized travel agencies that work with disabled travelers. Whether you work with a specialized agency or make plans on your own, it is important not to over-plan each day.

When I talk about mobility devices, most people think of a wheelchair. A mobility device can include walkers, canes, wheelchairs, and scooters. Many people who have balance issues, and or muscle weakness depend on mobility devices for ambulation. As an occupational therapist, I have seen many people use various mobility devices while traveling across the globe. I have seen people in wheelchairs go to the beach, take cruises, and participate in a wide variety of tours.

Mobility devices allow people to ambulate safely, however you are dependent on the amount of support the device offers, your level of coordination and strength, and many other factors. There are many tools and services that can be very helpful for travelers with disabilities. Here is a traveler's checklist that can assist you with your initial planning for your trip.

Disabled Travel Checklist

1. *Initially, you will want to think about what type of trip you will be taking. Think about your daily and weekly mobility requirements and how you get around.*

2. *Do you tire easily?*

3. *What kind of physical activities do you find difficult?*

4. *Do you find that climbing stairs make you tired? How many are you comfortable with?*

5. *Can you walk on an uneven pavement?*

6. *Walking for short distances? (Less than 10 minutes)*

7. *Walking for longer distances? (Over 30 minutes)*

8. *Can you stand for long periods of time?*

9. *What type of equipment do you use to improve your mobility?*

10. *Do you have a hearing impairment?*

11. *Do you have a visual impairment?*

12. *Do you require oxygen?*

13. *Do you wear a pacemaker or cardioverter-defibrillator (ICD)?*

14. *Do you take medications?*

Chapter 2: Traveling with Mobility Devices

Walkers:

There are many types of walkers that are available, such as standard walkers which provide the most support and have no wheels or wheeled walkers which have 2 or 4 wheels at the bottom. There are some walkers that have a carry pouch or basket to carry small items. These devices fold and are very portable.

Canes:

Canes can be a wonderful tool to have available. Some individuals use one cane, and others navigate using two canes. Some canes can fold, have four legs, and many others can be very handy for hiking trips. One of my clients who had both knees replaced in his 70's, uses his cane on hikes throughout Australia and most recently Canada. He said it took several trips throughout the United States before he was comfortable venturing to other countries.

Wheelchairs:

If you travel with a wheelchair or scooter, make sure your scooter is in excellent working order before leaving home. It's great to get a tune-up and a general checkup to avoid breakdown and the inconvenience of being without your wheelchair when traveling. You should always mark your wheelchair and all removable parts before leaving home if you are traveling domestically. You should use a label with your name and a post office box address for security reasons.

There are two different types of wheelchairs, one type of chair is the standard manual, and the other is motorized. Standard manual chairs allow the user to propel them forward and backward. Some of the manual chairs have leg rests, footplates, and head supports. Standard chairs can be ultra-light or have a heavy duty frame construction.

When you are traveling, it can be very convenient to have a chair that has a folding frame. In general the lighter the weight of the chair the greater the ease of use. Some ultra-light models are customized for the user to participate in sports, such as tennis and racing. There are wheelchairs with specialized wheels that can be used on the sand at the beach. It will take some planning, but it is possible to enjoy the beach while relaxing in a specialized wheelchair.

Motorized or power wheelchairs can be customized with some different options, such as reclining backs, tilt-in-space for pressure relief for an individual who has spasms, or has a spinal cord injury, and utilizes specialized pneumatic tires. If your wheelchair has specialized pneumatic tires, you should pack a repair kit in your carry-on bag just in case of a problem.

I had a client who loved the theatre, however after his accident, he was soon confined to a wheelchair; and realized not all cities are the same regarding wheelchair accessibility. He continues to go to the theatre; however, he has mentioned that some cities in the United States are very difficult to navigate in a wheelchair, even with the passage of the American with Disabilities Act (ADA). In the United States, the American with Disabilities Act allows public and privately owned businesses that serve the public from discriminating against individuals with disabilities.

What resources are available to assist passengers with disabilities who are traveling by air?

When you book your flights, it is important to make sure the reservationist knows that you will need wheelchair assistance. It's a good idea to have the airport attendant transport you to and from your flight which can save you a significant amount of time and energy. The airport attendant knows where all the gates are and if you need to go through customs, the attendant will push you to the head of the line.

If you are traveling by air, always contact your airline to confirm if they can handle your power wheelchair. You will want to re-confirm with an airline at least 48 hours and preferably 72 hours before departure to get maximum support at all airport terminals.

You will also want to contact the Transportation Security Administration (TSA) which was created after September 11, 2001, to strengthen the security of the nation's transportation systems and allow freedom of movement for all people. Travelers may call TSA Cares toll free at 1-855-787-2227 before traveling with questions about screening policies, procedures and what to expect at the security checkpoint.

TSA Cares is a helpful resource which has a live person available to answer questions specifically for passengers with disabilities, medical conditions or other circumstances. Traveling is all about planning and preparation, and it is critical to have a good resource to help you prepare for the screening processes before flying.

If one of the agents cannot answer your specific question, you will be referred to one of the disability experts. The hours of operation for the TSA Cares helpline are Monday through Friday 8 a.m. – 11 p.m. EST and weekends and Holidays 9 a.m. – 8 p.m. EST. Travelers who are deaf or hard of hearing can use a relay service to contact TSA Cares or can e-mail TSA-ContactCenter@dhs.gov.

Remember that TSA recommends that passengers call approximately 72 hours ahead of travel so that TSA Cares has the opportunity to coordinate checkpoint support with a TSA Customer Service Manager located at the airport when necessary.

You may want to inquire about wheelchair accessible vehicles if you are traveling by air or cruising. Once you arrive to your destination, you will need to have made prior arrangements especially if you will be covering a lot of ground.

There is a growing list of travel tours and many wheelchair accessible accommodations that have become very popular in the past 5 years.

What resources are available to assist passengers with disabilities who are traveling by train?

Amtrak is the major rail transport company in the United States and provides a variety of accommodations for travelers with disabilities. Here's a partial list below:

Reservations- If you need accessible bedroom accommodations and wheelchair space be sure you make your reservations early due to space limitations. Amtrak does not have assigned seating, but you can make an advanced request for lower level seating and position you close to accessible bathrooms.

If you will be traveling overnight, you will want to ask the reservation clerk about the Superliner and View-liner accessible bedroom features.

Boarding and Detraining- Many stations have high platforms that are level with the train door, and some have low-level platforms with station-board lifts. Currently, the weight limit with the lifts is 600 pounds.

Accommodations- Amtrak trains have assessable seating and one assessable bathroom in one coach car and sleeping car. Accessible seating includes space for a passenger with a wheelchair, transfer seat, and storage for the wheelchair.

What resources are available to assist passengers with disabilities who use wheelchairs that travel by bus?

Traveling by Greyhound is very accommodating for travelers with disabilities. Greyhound has Customers with Disabilities Assist Line, with agents who can be very helpful. Greyhound designates the front seats on either side of the coach are priority seating for people with disabilities. If you travel with any wheelchair, be sure to contact the Customers with Disabilities Assist Line for size, weight, and other limitations at (800) 752-4841.

Greyhound is very accommodating with boarding and de-boarding assistance. They offer wheelchair lift equipped busses, Scalamobils, and Aisle masters which can also offer alternative boarding assistance.

If you require a personal care assistant to travel with you, that assistant may be allowed to travel at no additional charge. Policies with Amtrak frequently change so you will want to verify if this benefit is still available. The tickets for your assistant are one-way only; however, you can request a return ticket on the day of travel.

What resources are available to assist passengers with disabilities who use wheelchairs that want to cruise?

There are many cruise-lines that are fully accessible to those traveling in wheelchairs. It may be very beneficial to seek a travel agency who specializes in dealing with people with disabilities. If you want to make your reservations, the following checklist can be helpful:

<u>Cruising Checklist</u>

1. *Are all levels of the ship accessible?*

2. *What are the dimensions of the entry doorway into your cabin and bathroom?*

3. *Are the restrooms outside of my cabin accessible with a wheelchair?*

4. *Are there grab bars installed next to the toilet and in the shower?*

5. *Will a shower seat be available?*

6. *Can I take my electric scooter aboard the ship? What are the requirements?*

7. *How accessible are the ports I want to visit?*

8. *Will accessible motor coaches be available or wheelchair lifts at each port of call?*

CHAPTER 3: TRAVELING WITH A HEARING IMPAIRMENT

The number of Americans with a hearing loss has doubled during the past 30 years. Data from a Federal survey estimated that there are over 40 million Americans who have a communication disability, and over 4 million individuals who rely on a Telecommunications Device for the Deaf (TDD).

A TDD consists of a keyboard, which holds 20-30 character keys on a screen and a modem. The device rings using a flashing light or via a watch with a vibrating wrist band. Some new TDD's have answering machines. Deaf individuals enjoy using a phone however they must know how to type.

Hearing callers can get in touch with a TDD user by utilizing a message relay center (MCR) to make the call anytime. The caller will call the (MCR) using a TDD or voice system and will speak to an experienced operator who will act as an interpreter. Toll-free (800)-627-3529

What are the common problems hearing impaired travelers face when they are away from home?

Some of the common problems include great difficulty hearing and understanding flight boarding and in-flight announcements. It is also difficult to hear clearly in the presence of background noise.

Despite the tremendous advances in hearing aid technology, understanding voices clearly in the presence of background noise remains a huge problem. Background noise includes traffic noise, music, a marching band, or voices such as children crying, can result in reverberation.

Reverberation causes sound to echo when reflected off room surfaces at airports, restaurants, or any place where people gather. Background noise can be overwhelming because it prevents or distracts you from listening to something you want to hear, such as last-minute flight information or where to purchase your tickets.

As a clinical Audiologist, most of my clients who are new to hearing aids often report the presence of background noise to be particularly bothersome during the first several weeks. Hearing loss in most cases is gradual and suddenly wearing new hearing aids is challenging because they may not have heard everyday noises such as dishes clattering, keys dropping, shoes walking on a hardwood floor at an amplified level for many years.

It takes time to get used to these new sounds, and you have to be patient with yourself. Research has shown that it can take up to 4-6 months to get used to wearing a hearing aid. Experienced hearing aid users still have difficulties with the very best technology; however, have had more experience in challenging listening situations.

The intercom systems available in the rail stations, airports, and live events do not always have the best reception. Hearing impaired travelers can be at a disadvantage and could miss gate connections and last minute announcements over the public intercom systems.

With technology changing rapidly what are some of the solutions hearing impaired travelers can use to improve their ability to hear?

In the past several years, hearing aids with directional microphones have been clinically proven to help reduce background noise and increase the speech signal. Directional microphones in most hearing aids have to be activated by using your fingers or through remote control. Some hearing aids have automatic features which can adjust to a variety of environments.

Directional microphones allow you to hear the speech signal in front while reducing the presence of background noise from behind. Directional microphones can work well when you are attending a lecture or in a noisy restaurant. Please keep in mind, they don't eliminate background noise, and some establishments have poor architectural designs that make it difficult to understand speech.

Another solution is utilizing FM transmitters, which picks up a speakers voice and transmits this to the listener's ear. FM technology can be very useful because the FM transmitter favors sounds that are very close to it, resulting in hearing the talker's voice at a level that is significantly louder than the noise. In the clinical studies, it was found that people enjoyed the use of FM systems because they now find speech significantly easier to understand.

There are also digitally modulated (DM) assistive listening devices which filter background noise and greatly enhance speech. These devices have small receiver and allow full participation in all situations. Comfort Audio is the leader of cutting-edge products utilized in school systems, boardrooms, and personal use.

There have been many studies that have demonstrated the effectiveness of listening training for adults with hearing loss. Here are two training programs that are now available: The Sensimetrics Seeing and Hearing Speech and the Listening Auditory Communication Enhancement program (LACE). The clinical studies continue to show very positive results for both programs. For more information be sure to take a look at the resource list.

What is Blue Tooth and how can TV Communications be improved?

Even with the very best of technology, certain communication needs cannot be solved by the use of hearing aids alone. These situations can include the use of telephone, alarm clock, doorbell, smoke detector, television, and radio.

Many have heard about the use of TV EARs. TV Ears are designed for listening to the TV without interference from surrounding noise or the need to use very high volume. My clients have convinced me that the ability to reduce the sound from the TV with a simple headset, while others are in the room with normal hearing has saved their marriage! There are many models available for use with or without the hearing aids.

What can I do to hear better on the telephone?

Telephone amplifying devices are very popular, and many standard telephone receivers are not hearing aid compatible. When shopping for a new telephone make sure the phone is hearing aid compatible. There are cordless and corded devices. In order to use a hearing aid compatible phone your hearing aid must have a t-coil. The t-coil eliminates the sounds from your environment and only picks up sounds from the telephone. The T-coil is automatically activated in some hearing aids, and others must manually activate it to work properly.

If you continue to struggle or know someone who has difficulty with the phone, Caption Call may be the answer. With Caption call, you can understand every word of the phone call because there is a large display of what the callers say. To qualify you to need a high-speed internet connection, a home phone connection, and electrical outlet. Sorenson Communications is the leader in telecommunication relay services and will provide free delivery, free installation, and free captioning service for those who qualify. All details including the free phone promo code will be provided in the resource section. Please keep in mind information about phones is constantly being updated.

Communicating on cellular phones can be challenging in some situations. There are many manufacturers and its best to talk to your Audiologist before buying a new cellular phone to find out the best system to meet your needs.

What's all this talk about Bluetooth?

Bluetooth and wireless technology have become increasingly popular. New hearing aids can transmit sound from Bluetooth devices, such as

Bluetooth cell phones. There hearing aids require an interface that wirelessly picks up the Bluetooth signal from Bluetooth-compatible devices and transmits the signal to the hearing aid. The cool thing about it is that you don't have to hold the phone to your ear or hearing aid to hear the sounds. You can wirelessly stream sound from a TV, cellular phone, PC and even a person into your hearing aids!

The use of remote controls with hearing aids is also on the rise. Remote controls allow the user to make volume control, program adjustments, and other changes discreetly without touching the hearing aids. Today, there are many options available, and everything all starts with the hearing evaluation and personal needs analysis with your Clinical Audiologist.

Do I have tinnitus which is that awful ringing in my ear....what can be done about it?

According to the National Institute on Deafness and other Communications Disorders, over 25 million Americans suffer from tinnitus. Researchers have been searching for a cure, and for many tinnitus sufferers the sounds it creates in their ears can be debilitating. Doctors attempt to identify and treat the underlying cause.

There are some tinnitus treatment options which do require an investment of time and personal effort to be effective. There has been some information on alternative treatments such as herbal preparations and various procedures such as acupuncture, hyperbaric oxygen, and even hypnosis that have also been used with varying results. Reducing or avoiding caffeine and salt intake has helped many relieve their tinnitus symptoms, while others have used behavioral and cognitive therapies.

When you have tinnitus it is important to get a hearing and tinnitus evaluation. The truth of the matter is that 1 out of 6 Americans suffer from this and over 50% of the individuals with tinnitus also have hearing loss. There has been considerable evidence that sound therapy is one of the most effective methods of treatment for people with tinnitus.

Be sure to speak with your Clinical Audiologist or Hearing Aid Dispenser about the most current options available for tinnitus.

What's all the hype about these hearing Loop Systems, how do they enhance your hearing?

If you have felt left out at the symphony or while attending the theatre, you are not alone. There is a growing group of consumers who won't go to the museums or theatres because they have difficulty hearing. Some of the theatres offer specialized headsets which are designed to enhance the user's ability to hear. Many consumers have complained and criticized these systems due to the poor sound quality, static, and interference.

Hearing loop systems utilize a simple technology that has been around for decades, as a means of relaying signals from a telephone to a receiver called a telecoil or t-coils. T-coils are now readily placed in many hearing aids and all cochlear implants. Once you activate the telecoil in your hearing aid, you can experience a clear, non-distorted and directed sound to the end user.

In Europe, this technology is widely available and has been very well received, however very slow to adopt in the United States. Many cities in North America have been starting to utilize this technology which is presently being installed in museums, banks, libraries, ticket counters, stores, and many other public places.

One of my clients was going to cancel her subscription to the theatre because she had become increasingly frustrated with not being able to hear clearly. Although she had hearing aids with a t-coil, the theatre she preferred did not have the loop system. She recently contacted me and was overjoyed that her theatre installed the loop system, and for the first time she could hear the performance very clearly.

Can you provide the best strategies to use when you are hearing impaired?

Communication Strategies Top 10 Checklist:

1. *When calling for reservations, tell the reservation clerk that you are hearing impaired and that you would prefer to sit in a booth. Sitting at a table in the middle of the restaurant can be very challenging due to the sound being all around you.*

2. *You will want to pick a table in the quietest section of the restaurant away from the bar and kitchen and make sure the lighting at the table is adequate.*

3. *Make reservations ahead of time and try to select times where the restaurant is not as crowded.*

4. *Try to selecting restaurants where you won't be bombarded with noise, such as a sports bar or during the play-off games when the restaurant is crowded.*

5. *If the background music is loud, you can request that the music is turned down.*

6. *Make sure you tell the waitress that you have a hearing loss and to ask for them to speak up when talking as well, and to slow down the rate of speech.*

7. *Try to limit the number of dining partners so that you can focus on the speech.*

8. *If you have hearing aids, use the directional microphone setting. This setting will help to reduce the presence of background noise, but remember this program setting will not eliminate it.*

9. *Many theatres and churches around the country are installing the induction loop system. In the induction loop system, you will need to set your hearing aids to the t-coil position to have a direct input of the speaker.*

10. *Always try to arrive early to an event so you can sit close to the sound source and to other important speakers.*

Tracey Ingram, M.A., M.S.

Be sure to get your hearing evaluated annually. If you are leaving town, make sure you get your hearing aids checked with your Audiologist or Hearing dispenser before leaving. You will want to do this at least two weeks before leaving so if the hearing aid has to be sent to the manufacturer, you will have it back in time for travel.

How do I prepare for traveling to the airport with my new hearing aids?

It is recommended that passengers who are deaf or hearing impaired notify a TSA security officer of any assistance needed especially if you are wearing a cochlear implant or hearing aids. If you need special assistance communicating such as augmentative communication board, or sign language, be sure to inform the security officer before screening.

Passengers can be screened using imaging technology or walk-through metal detectors without removing your device. If you decide you do not want to use image technology, please inform the security officer and a pat-down or manual inspection may be required. The devices may need to be screened manually if they are in your carry-on bags. You will want to allow for extra time for these procedures.

When you arrive at the gate, be sure to inform the flight attendants that you are hearing impaired. You can request that the airline staff inform you personally as soon as information is announced regarding your flight. Some airlines will allow deaf passengers to board first so the cabin crew can review safety procedures before other passengers arriving.

Chapter 4: Traveling with a Visual Impairment

A person with a visual impairment has significant limitation of visual capability resulting from disease, trauma, degenerative, or congenital problems that cannot be corrected by medical interventions. There are individuals with low vision who may wear corrective lenses and still may have considerable difficulty.

There are also levels of visual field impairments that include loss of central and peripheral vision. When you think about it, anyone with reduced vision not corrected by glasses or contact lenses can be considered to be visually impaired. Globally, in 2002, more than 161 million people were classified with a visual impairment, with greater than 124 million classified with low vision and 37 million were legally blind.

What are the types of Assistive Technology available?

Many people who fall in the low vision category can use their residual vision to complete their daily tasks without the use of technology. There are low vision specialists who can help the individual maximize the functional level of a patient's vision.

They may suggest the use of electronic magnification for near tasks. It can be very helpful, to begin with, a technology assessment. The types and amount of assistive technology have grown tremendously over the years.

Assistive technology comes in many forms and falls in the category of low technology such as using a portable hand-held electronic magnifier, such as the "Pebble", to read maps or travel brochures, to high technology such as using computers with voice recognition software.

To view distant images such as a visit to an art museum or other far away images, there are electronic telescopes available. Auditory software is also available such as talking calculators and programs that convert text to voice or Braille. Keep an eye on new trends because products often become discontinued and new items become available.

If you need a low vision magnifier, you will want to take the time to explore the vast array of choices available in lenses, video camera magnifiers, and lighting. Always think about your budget, goals, and what features you would like before your consultation with a low vision specialist. Ask yourself the question: "What exactly are my needs and what do I want the device to do for me", can save you a lot of time when you are shopping.

It is important to realize that one size does not fit all when it comes to low vision devices. A person who has permanent blind spots in their visual field may need a different type of magnifier than a person with a peripheral vision loss. Low vision magnifiers are available in these categories:

a.   Video camera magnifiers & Telescopes

b.   Handheld or stand magnifiers

c.   Magnifiers mounted on eyeglasses

d.   Low vision reading glasses

It's important to remember that every device has advantages and disadvantages. When you sit down with a vision specialist, they will help you choose a device that meets your goals and your requirements. They will also show you alternatives. Your eye condition may be more complicated than what is detected by an eye test. For example, you could develop a loss of night vision or find it difficult to see objects against backgrounds of similar colors.

If you are an avid reader, you may find that you need a magnifier that can help you sustain concentration for an extended period with an expanded field of view. You will also want the ability to scan ahead to process information quickly. Various lenses and powers in the same device may be useful to do a variety of different tasks.

A magnifier with 6x power has a disadvantage because you will see a much smaller area than a 3x magnifier. You will want a magnifier with the least power you can get away with to see the largest area. Always ask yourself what specific tasks are you are going to be doing with that device.

If you are going to spend over $500 for a low vision device you will definitely want to make an appointment with a low vision expert who can advise you, let you try out the devices before committing to a purchase, and to be able to return the device for a refund in a reasonable period of time if it does not work for you. You will want to be able to have a warranty in case if something goes wrong with the device. It's important to stick with reputable companies that are established.

What are the options available when traveling?

Many visually impaired travelers utilize tour groups. There are several companies that specialize in blind tours. Tour groups can be very helpful, and most tour group leaders have had some disability awareness training. The nice bonus about the tour groups is that everything is arranged for you. If possible, try to stay connected via the internet if you choose to travel outside of a tour group.

Internet cafes can be limited for people who are visually impaired. One solution is to utilize "Zoom Text" software which will customize the magnification and font/color. This can be useful for an individual who is also color blind.

Zoom text software also has audio features as well. "Zoom Text" can help you navigate and find things on webpages, and with the recording option, it can allow you to turn text from documents, emails, and webpages into audio recordings. These audio recordings can be wonderful for travel because they can be transferred to your mobile device to listen at your convenience. Information on the "Pebble" and "Zoom Text software" is available in the resource section.

Visually impaired Traveler Top 8 "On the go strategies."

1. *When planning a trip be sure to have directions written down before leaving, especially if you cannot read them. You can use this by showing the written information to someone else if you get lost. It's also a great idea to have a copy of the exact address of your destination.*

2. *Be sure to inform everyone including the travel agency, hotel, and all travel partners about the fact you are visually impaired. Be sure to be very upfront about your visual limitations.*

3. *Don't be afraid to ask for help. If you cannot see a monitor or a sign, be sure to ask a police officer or customer service representative to assist.*

4. *Always carry the most important necessities in your carryons, such as your money, medication, keys, tickets, and essentials.*

5. *Be sure to carry your cane. The cane easily identifies you as visually impaired.*

6. *Always ask for discounts. You might be pleasantly surprised about many tourist attractions give significant discounts for visually impaired travelers and their companions.*

7. *Be sure to research accommodations and destinations before your arrival.*

8. *Enhance your sensory experience by going on tours that will allow you to touch objects.*

How does one travel with a service animal?

According to the Americans with Disabilities Act businesses, such as restaurants, hotels, stores, airlines, must allow people with disabilities to bring their Guide dogs with them. Under the ADA a service animal is defined as any dog trained to perform a task for the blind, hearing impaired, alerting others to an oncoming seizure and many more.

Therapy dogs who provide emotional support or companionship as prescribed by a medical doctor are not classified as service animals under the ADA and not eligible to access public places.

There are some countries that don't allow guide dogs or have quarantine requirements. Hawaii now allows Guide dogs, but there are very strict and complex rules and regulations for entry. To visit the Hawaiian Islands with a Guide dog will require months of planning.

When making hotel arrangements be upfront to inform them that you will be accompanied by a service dog. Remember it is unlawful for businesses to assess an extra fee or deposit because of your service animal.

Although you don't have to leave a deposit, you are responsible for any damage caused by your dog. If your dog is snarling, barking excessively and threatening other guests, the dog may be excluded from the premises. Always plan ahead, and you can have an amazing travel experience with your service animal.

How do I prepare for traveling to the airport with a visual impairment and service animal?

When traveling with your service animal be sure to have the appropriate identification and papers in your carryon bag. This includes documentation, a harness, proof of vaccinations, and health certificates.

When you are booking your ticket be sure to inform the agent that your service dog will accompany you in the main cabin. Finding the right seat is important because the animal cannot block an aisle or be in an area blocked off for evacuation purposes.

Make sure your dog has been relieved before boarding. Do not feed the dog or sedate the dog before flying. Pre-boarding allows you to find an ideal seat and get comfortable before taking off.

If you are visually impaired, notify a TSA security officer and inform them about your situation and discuss the type of assistance you require to complete the screening process. You can be screened using imaging technology as long as you don't have a service animal. If you cannot or refuse to be screened by imaging technology you will be screened using a pat down and inspection procedure.

Any assistive technology such as Braille note-takers, specialized computer monitors, telescopes will need to undergo X-ray screening unless they are too large. If the item it too large it will be inspected by an officer.

Chapter 5: Traveling with Oxygen

People who have severe lung diseases, such as chronic obstructive pulmonary disease (COPD), emphysema, or shortness of breath often will rely on supplemental oxygen. Many research studies have shown an increase in survival rates from people who use oxygen greater than 14 hours daily and can allow individuals do normal activities.

In general, you will want to avoid traveling in high elevations, extreme temperatures, and very humid environments because of increased difficulty breathing. You will want to have several copies of a physician's statement with you who can specify your general condition and ability to travel, the need for medical oxygen, oxygen flow rate and duration of oxygen requirements. The letter should also contain the doctor's address, office and after-hours telephone numbers, and a fax number.

How do I use Oxygen Safely?

Although oxygen is a safe gas and is nonflammable, traveling with oxygen can be very intimidating for the inexperienced. It is very important to plan ahead and follow general oxygen safety guidelines. Here are some helpful tips recommended by the American Lung Association.

1. *It is important to not use oxygen around open flames, such as cigarettes, cigars, lighters, matches, or candles.*

2. *It is critical that you not use oxygen around other sources of heat, such as electric or gas heaters and/or stoves.*

3. *If you are using supplemental oxygen, avoid using creams, lotions, or any products containing petroleum — the combustion of flammable products containing petroleum can also be supported by the presence of oxygen.*

4. *Oxygen cylinders need to be stored safely in a secure, upright position in an approved place for storage.*

5. *When not in use oxygen values need to be turned off.*

6. *Pay close attention to the safety instructions recommended by your oxygen supply company, regarding any safety precautions while using supplemental oxygen.*

Are there any special guidelines I need to take while riding on Amtrak?

It is important when you are making reservations that you notify Amtrak that you are bringing oxygen on board at least 12 hours in advance or greater. You will also want to confirm your reservation 24-48 hours before leaving. While traveling on Amtrak your oxygen equipment can be brought on board, but you must advise the conductor that you are carrying oxygen when you board the train.

You will need to provide a battery backup power source of at least 12 hours that does not require the use of on-board electrical power. Your oxygen tanks and associated equipment must be Underwriter's Laboratory (U.L) or Factory Mutual (F.M.) listed. You must remember that you can have no more than two 75 pound tanks or six 20 pound tanks per person. The tanks must be separated and handled individually.

When planning your trip, be aware of the total trip time so you can make sure you have more than an adequate supply. It would be wise to plan for delays and bring at least 25% additional supply of oxygen.

If you cannot bring enough oxygen, it is critical for you to arrange with oxygen supply companies to re-supply you en-route. You will want to make sure your reservation agent informs you about the stops en-route and how much time you will have at each station to make sure you have more than enough time to allow for the oxygen delivery.

Amtrak requires that the oxygen tanks stored on board must have the wheels removed. When moving around the train make sure that you are not in or near any smoking area with oxygen tanks. Once you have arrived at your destination, you will have to make separate arrangements for oxygen.

Be sure to ask the reservation agent because they belong to a network of local oxygen suppliers. Travel safe with confidence. Never run low on traveling with oxygen again by utilizing Advanced Aeromedical or Travel o2 which are listed in the resource section.

Are the guidelines for travel different when traveling by air?

The Federal Aviation Administration (FAA) requires a physician's statement which details your oxygen needs to fly on a commercial airline. The FAA regulations are subject to change without notice. For the most current guidelines, you will want to contact the airline you will be using. This information supplied in this book are general guidelines.

The FAA forbids the use of privately supplied oxygen, and you must use the oxygen supplied by the airline that you are flying. The airlines can support your oxygen equipment provided it meets certain labeling requirements set by the carrier. You will need to contact the airline that you are using in advance because they all have their policies and procedures.

Most airlines will require a letter from your physician that will have to be approved. Please keep in mind the airline will charge an extra fee to cover the oxygen they provide. It is best to have a direct flight whenever possible. Some airlines will charge per each leg of the flight. If you have to change planes on your trip, you could potentially be charged twice.

Airlines also do not provide oxygen for in-terminal use. If you are making a connection or have a layover between flights, you will need to make oxygen arrangements from an outside supplier.

How will I be able to cruise?

Each cruise line will have different requirements for traveling with oxygen. Advanced notice of at least ten days is required. You will also want to have a letter from your doctor describing your condition to travel, oxygen dosage required, and a statement that you require medical oxygen. It is important to contact the medical department of the cruise-line so your medical conditions can be evaluated. Once you have approval from the medical department, you can now make your reservations.

It is a requirement for you to arrange with an oxygen supplier and the cruise-line delivery and on-board storage of your oxygen. If you are interested in shore excursions, you will have to make another arrangement because oxygen from the ship cannot accompany you ashore. Many cruise lines have a lot of restrictions with oxygen and can charge very high prices so you will want to allow time to plan.

How can I travel by Greyhound?

It is important that you make your arrangements as far in advance as possible and inform the agent in the Customer relations department that you will be traveling with oxygen. The customer relations department has a copy of their policy for passengers traveling with oxygen.

How can I travel by Automobile?

When traveling by automobile you will have a lot more flexibility. You will need to consider the following: length of trip, length of each day's drive, the number of overnight stops, and rest stops. In general, you will want to avoid driving through areas with high elevations. You will not want to store your oxygen tanks in your vehicle if the temperature exceeds 120 degrees Fahrenheit.

CHAPTER 6: TRAVELING WITH MEDICATIONS

If you take prescription medication, it is important that you pack all of your essential medications in your carry-on bag. Be sure to have extra medicine in your checked bag in case if you are delayed. If you have diabetes and use insulin, bring several unopened vials and store them in at least two or three places.

You should also carry a laminated copy of all of your prescriptions, and a letter from your doctor which describes your medications, diagnosis, and all of your requirements. The letter should also contain the physicians first and last name, phone numbers, and emergency contact information.

Be sure to ask your pharmacy or physician for the generic equivalent name of your prescriptions in case you need to purchase additional medication abroad. Travel with all of your medication in their labeled containers. Take a copy of your immunization records and your health insurance card.

What are some extra precautions I need to take while traveling by air?

Medically necessary liquids are allowed through a checkpoint in any amount once they have been screened. Keep your laminated copy of all your prescriptions handy to show a TSA security officer if needed. You will want to limit the amount of liquid to what is reasonably necessary for the flight.

Liquids, gels, and aerosols are screened by X-ray, and medically necessary items more than 3.4 ounces will receive additional screening a passenger could be asked to open the liquid or gel for additional screening. You will want to inform the TSA officer if you do not want your liquid gels or other medical aerosols to be X-rayed. The TSA most likely will provide additional screening of you and your property, which may include a pat-down and manual inspections.

The accessories required to keep your medically necessary liquids cool - such as freezer packs or frozen gel packs – are permitted through the screening checkpoint and may be subject to additional screening. These accessories are treated as liquids unless they are frozen solid at the checkpoint. If these accessories are partially frozen or slushy, they are subject to the same screening as other liquids and gels.

Be sure to declare your medical items to an officer and separate them from other items before the screening process. Supplies that are associated with medically necessary liquids and gels – such as IV bags, pumps, and syringes are allowed through a checkpoint once they have been screened by X-ray or inspection.

CHAPTER 7: FITNESS ON THE ROAD

Traveling always presents a change in your normal schedule or routine. Your fitness plan often will suffer, but with a little planning you can bring your exercise on the road and stay fit. Here are some helpful tips.

1. It's a nice benefit if there is a hotel gym handy. Studies have shown that exercising while traveling can improve your reaction and alertness by up to 61%. Exercising doesn't have to be complicated. When you are making your hotel reservations or the travel agent, be sure to inquire about the availability of a gym at the hotel/lodging or nearby and make a plan to use it.

2. If the gym is not available, you can always inquire about walking trails. Some hotels have walking trails on the property or adjacent. Many have a concierge and will have fitness trail maps available for free if you inquire. Anytime you can get outside and get moving whether you are in a wheelchair, using a walker or cane, or ambulatory can offer some healthy benefits such as a reduction in stress.

3. Portable exercise equipment is ideal, and you will never miss a workout again. Pick up a set of resistance bands. Resistance bands can be used to increase circulation, strengthen lower and upper body muscles, and increase the range of motion. They are typically packaged with three levels of resistance (light, medium, heavy). You can try these <u>resistance bands</u> which are less than $10.00 in the U.S at the time this book was published.

4. Swimming on the go is possible if you do a little research beforehand into pool locations, schedules, and fees, you'll be better prepared upon arrival. Don't forget to pack a <u>tether cord</u> which is a training tool when you find out that Olympic sized pool you

read about in the hotel promo is no larger than a large bathtub. A tether cord is a thick bungee cord that attaches to a fixed object at the end of the pool, such as a ladder and a harness on the other end that you attach to yourself. This provides resistance and stretches but keeps you swimming in the same spot which will keep you in swim shape.

CHAPTER 8: THE DIABETIC TRAVELER

Diabetes mellitus (DM) is a worldwide epidemic and is one of the most challenging health problems in the 21st century. According to the World Health Organization (WHO), 366 million people had diabetes in 2011, and by 2030 this will have risen to 552 million. The number of people with type 2 diabetes is increasing rapidly in every country. There are over 183 million with diabetes who are undiagnosed.

How do I prepare myself for a trip if I am a type 2 diabetic?

If you are thinking about going on a trip, you have to think ahead to handle your diabetes. Before a long trip is sure to have a medical exam to make sure your diabetes is under control and ask your doctor for a signed letter on their letterhead, with all of the contact information listed. The letter should describe your medications, diagnosis, all of your requirements including your prescriptions.

If you are going on a trip that is two or more weeks and out of the country, you will need to prepare for an emergency. Be sure to wear your medical identification bracelet or necklace that shows you have diabetes. If an emergency occurs and you don't know where to go, try to reach the American consulate, the Red Cross, or local medical schools.

Depending on where you go, you may need a vaccination or immunization which is likely to affect your glucose or insulin balance. If you are injecting on an airplane, please note the pressure is different than on the ground which makes it difficult to measure insulin accurately. Do not inject air into the insulin bottle while in the pressurized cabin.

Take extra medications with you in your carry-on bag along with your doctor's laminated letter and prescriptions. Along with your carry-on bag, you need to have some appropriate snacks with you such as peanut butter, fruit, cheese, and crackers. Always assume the airport or airlines do not have appropriate food and pack your nutritious foods to take with you.

Always watch what you eat and if you are unfamiliar with the food item, be sure to ask for the list of the ingredients. Drink plenty of bottled water and not tap water when you are overseas.

If you are taking insulin shots and crossing time zones be sure to talk to your doctor before the trip to get some guidelines of how to plan the timing of your injections. Also, check your blood glucose levels while traveling is important as it is when you are at home. Jet lag can play tricks on you, and it can be hard to determine if your blood glucose is high or low.

Be sure to pack appropriate foot gear. Bring at least two pairs of shoes so you can change shoes often if you are going on a long trip. Be sure to pack a first aid kit to treat minor foot injuries immediately and do not go barefoot. Wear shoes appropriate for the activity you are participating in and whatever you do, do not wear open-toe shoes. You will increase your risk of injury and infection when the toes are exposed.

What is the role of exercise and diabetes management?

The research has consistently demonstrated that aerobic exercise helps to improve glucose control and enhanced insulin sensitivity. The American Diabetes Association (ADA) have made recommendations for type 2 diabetics to perform 30 minutes of vigorous aerobic exercise for 3x per week. The problem with this recommendation is that many severely obese, arthritic, severely disabled people have difficulty adhering to the vigorous schedule. The new guidelines of the ADA also include strength training as well, stating that resistance exercise is as important as aerobics. Before starting any exercise program be sure to check with your physician.

Resistance training has been reported to have some of the same benefits as aerobic exercise. In fact, the research shows that doing both resistance training (using weights or resistance bands) and aerobic training is essential to improve blood sugar levels and can have a profound impact on helping adults manage their diabetes. Resistance training also has the potential for increased muscle strength and bone density.

Chapter 9: Arthritis and Traveling

Arthritis affects over 50 million Americans and is an often a misunderstood disease. Arthritis is the leading cause of disability in the United States and frequently causes activity limitations. Keep in mind that arthritis is a blanket term for over 100 different conditions and diseases.

Arthritis can take many forms, and three of the most common are: Rheumatoid Arthritis (RA), Osteoarthritis (OA), and Juvenile Arthritis (JA). Participation in daily activities with individuals with RA or OA can vary from person to person. It is important to incorporate joint protection into all activities of daily living to help minimize pain.

Helpful Products

When you have arthritis, it's nice to know about products that can make your life easier and have been approved by the Arthritis Foundation for "ease of use".

Be sure to check out products by <u>IMAK Compression</u>. Imak Compression products are specifically designed to help reduce swelling, improve circulation, and provide added warmth to the affected area. Be sure to review their website for helpful products.

How can I manage my Arthritis when I'm on the go?

Traveling can be a great way to visit friends and see the world but for people with arthritis sitting for long periods of time can result in very stiff joints, fatigue, and stress on the joints. There are several ways to minimize stress on the joints which means you will need to plan.

If you are traveling by air, try to book non-stop to eliminate transfers and ask for a seat in an exit row, so you have more room. You can have your large bags shipped ahead of time to their destination to avoid carrying large bags to the airport. You can simply arrive at the airport with your carry-on bag with medications and snacks.

When traveling consider traveling during the weekdays if you have the choice because the airports, bus and rail terminals are less crowded. Be sure to take along inflatable pillows, ear plugs, small meals, or items that can make your trip more comfortable. You will want to stretch regularly to avoid unnecessary stiffness.

If you are traveling with a wheelchair and by car, you have the most flexibility and can arrange to stop every hour or so to do some stretching exercises. There are also cruise opportunities as well, which can be less fatiguing. The ships often offer stretching exercises and activities on board to help you stay in shape.

Exercise is essential for arthritis and helps increase energy levels, develops a better sleep pattern, maintains a healthy heart, decreases stress, and improves your self-esteem. As always, contact your physician before beginning any exercise program.

What are the best types of exercise I can do for my arthritis?

Aerobic and Endurance Exercises

Endurance exercises are physical activities that bring your heart up to the optimal range for 20-30 minutes. Endurance exercises are ideally performed 3x or more a week. Not all people can handle this level of activity especially when the joints are stiff and painful.

Keep in mind endurance exercises have to be chosen carefully for all patients with arthritis to avoid joint injury and pain. Swimming, cycling, and power walking are all examples of endurance exercises.

Resistance/Strengthening Exercises

The American Arthritis Foundation recommends the use of resistance band training as a safe and effective method to provide resistance, mobility, strengthen the muscles, and improved flexibility. Remember strength training, particularly in conjunction with regular aerobic exercise, can have a profound impact on a person's mental and emotional health.

Strengthening exercises can help with the restoration of balance and reduction of falls. There have been several studies that reveal that people who are involved with strength and balance training that are aged 60 and older show a reduction of falls and increased bone density.

Range of Motion Exercises

Ranges of motion exercises are beneficial for added flexibility and to prevent stiffness. Tai chi is an example of an exercise that will increase flexibility, posture, and balance. Tai-chi also falls into the category of an endurance exercise because it will improve your cardiovascular health and increase your aerobic capacity.

Yoga and Pilates can provide pain relief, relax stiff muscles, and ease sore joints with controlled movements. The stretches with yoga can improve your range of motion. Be sure not avoid exercising when your disease activity is flaring, and joints are inflamed.

The Arthritis Foundation has wonderful fitness programs which are designed to reduce pain, increase your flexibility, and help you live a better life with arthritis. They have a walk with ease program, tai chi, aquatic and other programs. To learn more about these programs in your area you can contact your local Arthritis Foundation office or visit www.arthritis.org.

Accessible travel resources for people with disabilities

Here is a partial list of resources available to you to help you plan your trip and prepare you for what you can expect as someone traveling with a disability. It is important to do due diligence when selecting an agency or service to assist you with your traveling itinerary. Each volume of this series will have updates and additional resources listed. If you know about great websites that can help travelers with disabilities, please let me know.

Airline Information & Consumer Information

Transportation Security Administration (TSA) – TSA secures the nation's airports and screens passengers and luggage

TSA Cares Special needs Website for travelers with disabilities - Phone number.   (866) 289-9673 (toll-free) – The hotline has operators available M-F 8am-11pm EST. Holidays and Weekends 9am-8pm EST.

Major Airlines
Alaska (800)252-7522
www.alaskaair.com

American (800)433-7300
www.aa.com

Continental (800)523-3273
www.continental.com

Delta (800)221-1212
www.delta.com

Northwest (800)225-2525
www.nwa.com

Southwest (800)435-9792
www.southwest.com

United (800)864-8331
www.united.com

US Airways (800) 428-4322
www.usairways.com

Cheaptickets - searches for best deals in airfares and lets you compare. See the section on travel planning trips for travelers with disabilities.

Bus Line & Railroad Security

Amtrak
http://www.amtrak.com

Rail Europe
www.raileurope.com

Greyhound Lines
 www.greyhound.com

Disability hotline for Greyhound customers
Voice (800)752-4841 (toll-free)
TDD/TTY (800) 345-3109 (toll-free)

Cruising Information

Cruisecritic.com A website that features a wide variety of cruising styles and has information on what to look for when traveling with specific disabilities.

Disabled world - Provides interesting reviews of accessible cruises, vacations, and tours.

Specialized Travel Agencies

Accessible Journeys
35 West Sellers Avenue
Ridley Park, PA. 19078
(800) 846-4537
www.accessiblejourneys.com

Easy Access Travel
5386 Arlington Avenue
Riverside, California. 92501
(800) 920-8989
www.easyaccesstravel.com

Flying Wheels Travel
143 W. Bridge Street
Owatonna, MN 55060
(507) 451-5005
www.flyingwheelstravel.com

Accessible Europe. A group of travel agents headquartered in Italy who specializes in accessible tourism. 011-39-011-30-1888. http://www.accessibleurope.com/

The American Society of Travel Agents (ASTA), 800-275-2783. Search for travel agents by specialty, including disability and accessible travel. www.asta.org

Specialized Resources

Access-able - Resources for senior travelers and travelers with special needs

Advanced Aeromedical – Coordinates medical oxygen and mobility products for traveling patients worldwide (24 hours a day). Call toll free (800)346-3556

American Diabetes Association – Leading the fight against the deadly consequences of diabetes and fighting for those affected with the disease. (312) 346-1805

Arthritis Foundation – A voluntary health agency covering all arthritis related conditions. (800) 283-7800

Apparelzed This site is aimed for people with spinal cord injuries; however there is lot of information for disabled travelers. There is an active forum and vibrant well-traveled community.

BrownMed.com – This site offers information about the distribution of IMAK Compression products for arthritis relief and other conditions.

Disabled travelers – An accessible and disability travel guide with home exchanges, a list of specialized travel agencies, and numerous other resources

Disabled world - Provides interesting travel tips and articles. Also contains links to disability-specific travel sites.

Haseltine Flyer - A handy wheelchair container which assures the maximum protection for air travel. Call (240) 476-7837

Mobility International USA - Resourceful website on a variety of specific disabilities, international exchange programs, and travel information.

Accessibility: Disabled World Travels

<u>SATH</u> – Society for Accessible Travel & Hospitality is a non-profit membership organization designed to raise awareness of the needs of travelers with disabilities.

List of 20 cities in the United States that are wheelchair friendly. A resource from the Christopher and Dana Reeve Foundation. <u>U.S. Wheelchair Friendly cities</u>

Travel Insurance: <u>www.insuremytrip.com</u> Website to purchase travel insurance, medical evacuation plans.

Travel Insurance Review: <u>Travel insurance reviews</u>. A website that is one of the best travel insurance resources

<u>The Luggage Club</u> – A free membership-based company that will pick up your luggage, wheelchair or other items and deliver them to your destination. Call toll-free (866) 289-9664. International (925) 627-8061.

<u>Travel o2</u> – Provider of oxygen services worldwide. Call toll-free (800)391-2041

<u>Trip advisor</u> - Provides an active disabled travelers' forum that also includes an Accessibility checklist for hotel accommodations.

<u>Wheelers</u> – A wheelchair accessible van rental service readily available at every major airport in the United States and over 300 additional locations. Call toll-free (800) 456-1371

Visually Impaired Resources

Pebble – Portable hand held electronic magnifier very suitable for traveling.

Zoom Text software – Amazing software that magnifies and changes font/color. There is also an audio component as well.

Comfort Audio – The leader in (DM) digitally modulated assistive listening products. Call toll free (888) 421-0843

Listening Auditory Communication Enhancement program (LACE) – LACE sill help you develop skills and strategies to improve your listening skills.

Message Relay Center (MCR) – 24-hour service available to relay telephone messages between a telephone user and TTY/TDD user. Toll-free (800)-627-3529

Phonak – Manufacturer of personal hearing aids and FM systems. Call toll free (800) 679-4871.

Sensimetrics Seeing and Hearing Speech – A program that uses the latest multimedia technology and personal computers to provide lip-reading training.

<u>Hearing Impaired Resources</u>

Caption Call – Sorenson Communications caption telecommunication device. Free promo code: ES1000. Get your free phone today for those who qualify, with free delivery and installation. <u>www.captioncall.com</u> (877) 557-2227

CapTel.com – The ultimate caption telecommunication device. There are many styles available. <u>www.Captel.com</u> (414) 921-1660

TV EARS   <u>www.TVears.com</u>

Affordable assistive listening device (Analog to Digital)   888 883-3277

Complaining and Your Rights

You deserve to have a wonderful holiday and get the treatment and services that you want, but sometimes there are problems that will occur. There are times where you feel like yelling and screaming which can make an embarrassing scene.

If you are assertive and find the person of authority to voice your complaints, try to explain the situation as best as you can. Please keep in mind that the process of finding a good compromise or solution can take time. If you are experiencing difficulty with air travel service you can contact the following:

U.S. Department of Transportation, Aviation Consumer Protection Division (ACPD)

24 hour hotline: Voice (202) 366-2220   TDD/TTY (202) 366-0511

The mailing address is helpful if you choose to write a letter which will be forwarded to an airline official:

Aviation Consumer Protection Division, C-75

U.S. Department of Transportation

1200 New Jersey Ave, S.E.

Washington, D.C. 20590

Every airline has a complaint resolution department available at the airport to discuss all problems that occurred while on the flight. Be sure to contact that individual as soon as possible to voice your concerns.

A Plea to your Very Generous Nature

If you have found this guide helpful in anyway and you like what you read, would you consider going to Amazon or Goodreads and leaving a review? The process is a lot easier than you think and I will be grateful. Simply click on the space below.

Keep in mind, I know you are busy, and I thank you for your kind words. I would be happy to reciprocate a favor for you, all you have to do is ask.

AMAZON REVIEW: https://www.amazon.com/review/create-review?ie=UTF8&asin=B00CPUHOLG&channel=glance-detail&ref_=cm_cr_dp_d_wr_but_top&#
Sincerely,
Tracey Ingram

ABOUT THE AUTHOR

Ms. Tracey Ingram, M.A., M.S. is a Clinical Audiologist and Occupational Therapist who presently is an author and healthcare consultant. She has written website copy and numerous written material blogs, small businesses, and agencies.

Check out my Author Blog: Travelingbarrierfree.com

Other points of note:

Ms. Ingram has been certified as an Accent Modification Specialist/ PESL Instructor and developed online accent modification classes for foreign professionals. She also has published the book and audio - *7 weeks to a Better American Accent for Native Mandarin Speakers©* in 2010

Don't forget to visit Sovereign Education Media Publishing Website and the Facebook page for current updates.

SOVEREIGN EDUCATION MEDIA

@TravelerswithDisabilities

Travelingbarrierfree.com